Women Should Never...

by Helena Owen and Clare Woodcock
Illustrated by Fran Orford

GW00402119

Nightingale Press

BATH

ISBN: 1903222 56 7

...sit in the back of the car
when their husband is driving.

...wear crushed velour
leisure suits.

...collect Pierrot dolls.

...commission large, misty,
sexy studio photographs
of themselves.

...wear saucy, off-the-shoulder milkmaid blouses.

...wear stirrup trousers.

...possess unbranded,
pink and white trainers.

...expose gnarled, discoloured toenails in sandals.

...wear the same clothes
as their mother for trips
out together.

...crave their mother's
hairstyles.

...declare that
The Edinburgh Woollen Mill
is their favourite shop.

...have moustaches.

...have tobacco-
stained fingers.

...wear petticoats that are
longer than their skirts.

...allow eyeliner
to clog their tear-ducts.

...wear plastic
clip-on earrings.

...wear miniskirts if they
have fat legs.

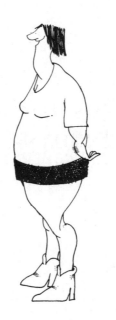

...reveal cracked,
hard skin in sling-back
sandals.

...wear skull rings.

...ask if they can inspect
their boyfriend's
septic sores.

...burst their boy-
friend's spots.

...refer to their pet cats
as 'the girls'.

...wear ankle socks to
mid-calf over tights.

...have love bites.

...carry clutch bags.

...wear diamond-
studded denim.

...wear earrings made
from feathers.

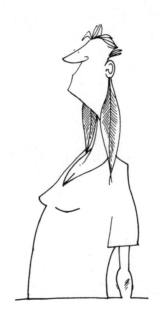

...dress babies in suits.

...wear a pocket watch.

...have side ponytails.

...wear their slippers
to the shops.

...call their husband 'my fella'.

...buy underwear from
Anne Summers.

...like underwear from
Anne Summers.

...be called Sian.

...assume baby
voices are sexy.

...wear stiletto heels
with jeans.

...wear football shirts.

...make their boyfriend's
wear the other half.

...miss evenings out
with friends in case
their boyfriend rings.

...wear any kind of
belted dress.

...shave their faces.

...wear their keys on a chain
hanging from their waistband.

...tuck jumpers into
their tights.

...propose to their boyfriend
on national television.

...wear pop socks with
knee-length skirts.

...wear jeans with
elasticated waistbands.

...wear legwarmers under
the illusion that they
are still in vogue.

...wear skin-tone tights
under jeans.

...fall asleep with a fag in
their hand.

...wear black, opaque tights
with white shoes.

...call their husband 'Dad'.

...stick their tongue out when they concentrate.

...carry small dogs in
shopping bags.

...have lipstick on their teeth.

...spit.

...pay for every date.

...wear golfing sweaters.

...wear broken-heart
necklaces.

...insist their husband wears
home-knit jumpers.

...wear seven-denier
tights if they haven't
shaved their legs.

...collect thimbles and
have a cabinet for them.

...knit body warmers
for their dogs.

...aspire to achieve
Madonna's Eighties' look.

...become a punk if they
are over sixty.

...call their husband
'my better half'.

...buy nightwear from Avon.

...pack for their boyfriend's
overnight trip.

...be impressed by a
Brewer's Fayre meal.

...ask a man if he's received
her Valentine's card.

...put love notes in their
husband's packed lunch.

...wear gold necklaces
that have their name
written in script.

...think it's a man's right to have his dinner on the table at five-thirty every day.

...perm their fringe.

...like shoes with kitten heels.

...insist their fiancé wear a
waistcoat to match the
bridesmaid's floral dress.

...have Jennifer Hart hair.

...wear heavily laced and
ill-fitting bras under blouses.

...jog without a sports bra.

...iron their husband's
Y-fronts.

...drink pints of Guinness.

...simply invent names for their children, like Caprina or Belvedere.

...buy clothes in a dress size smaller than they really are.

...wear blue mascara.

...wear sweaters with cute
kitten prints on them.

...buy chandeliers for
small houses.

...wear crocheted hats.

...shout abuse at the ref when
attending a football match.

...put a ribbon in their
dog's hair.

...wear black bras under
white tops.

...put their make-up on when driving down the motorway.

...feed their boyfriend
in public.

...name their children after
soap stars.

...listen to their mother's idea
of a suitable boyfriend.

...wear cute night-shirts.

...refer to their partner by their pet name in public.

...count calories during every meal and snack.

...wear thong leotards.

...have a "Love is..."
duvet cover.

...dress as wenches to
take part in medieval
battle re-enactions

...give their boyfriend a
piggyback.

...knit jumpers for
their favourite TV celebrities.

...play the trombone.

...talk about men's 'tackle'.

...talk about their
gynaecological history in
a post office queue.

...be happy for men to order
for them in restaurants.

...work with their husband
in a children's travelling
theatre company.

...admire the career of
Jeanette Krankie.

...fancy either of the
Chuckle Brothers.

...carry screw drivers
behind their ears.

...have brawls.

...say "my mate fancies you."

...keep a flip-chart at home to illustrate things to their family.

...use a laser pointer.

...hang net curtains over
garden shed windows.

...sniff a toddler's bottom
to check if it needs
to be changed.

...admit to doing a sick burp
on the first date.

...give demonstrations in village halls on spinning raw sheep's wool.

...talk wistfully about
weddings on a first date.